Old Wardour

Mark Girouard

Contents

Tour

EXTERIOR AND SETTING

Castles were originally military in purpose: located and designed to resist attack and dominate a town, major road or river crossing. But they were also lived in, often by a great person and his household, and so they acquired two distinct connotations: military and social status. A great man could therefore use the architecture of a castle to symbolize his dignity and rank in a building that had little, if any, military function.

England was at peace when Wardour was built, but the political situation was doubtful enough to call for a degree of security: small external windows on the lower floors, an entrance protected by portcullises, machicolations (openings in a parapet above an entrance, through which missiles could be dropped on attackers), and projecting towers for flanking fire.

But despite their military form, these features were intended, perhaps above all, to announce the presence of a great man, possibly the greatest in Wiltshire, for in other ways Wardour made little sense in terms of fortification. It was in a secluded place, of no military importance, set snugly below a hill instead of on top of it; it had no drawbridge, ditch or moat (its pond was for fish), and behind the entrance front it was topped by purely decorative turrets and cornice. It was, above all, the luxurious house, pleasantly situated, of a great man.

The present entrance by the ticket office and shop gives access to the open space around the castle through the massive

Above: The bust of Christ of the 1570s above the entrance. The inscription reads: 'Sub nomine tuo stet genus et domus' ('May the house and line stand firm under your name')

Below: Plan of Old Wardour showing the main features of the garden, the 14th-century hexagonal surrounding wall, and part of the terrace, which runs for a mile along the side of the hills through the woods

Facing page: The south-east wall and turret of Old Wardour; it is the only turret to have survived the more than 600 years since the castle was built

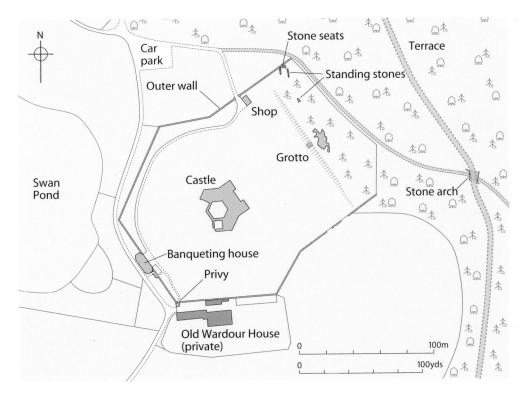

Plan labels: Car park · Stone seats · Terrace · Standing stones · Outer wall · Shop · Swan Pond · Grotto · Castle · Stone arch · Banqueting house · Privy · Old Wardour House (private) · N

0 — 100m
0 — 100yds

Above: The towering 14th-century façade of Old Wardour, with its single remaining turret visible on the left

Below: Cherry-pickers from a French handbook on health of about 1450. Wardour would originally have been surrounded by orchards, gardens, woodyard and stables

outer wall, which surrounds and echoes the plan of the castle (a hexagon with a rectangle added to one side). The spreading lawns, and the cedars and other conifers with which they are planted, date from landscaping in the mid 18th and early 19th centuries; originally there would have been a more workmanlike mix of gardens, orchard, woodyard, stable yard, and possibly farmyard, with stables and barns against the inside of the perimeter wall.

The wall is part of the original design – although rebuilt at least in part in the 16th century – but the entrance is not. Where the original entrance was is not known, but it was probably by way of a gatehouse in the rectangular projection of the outer wall, behind the 18th-century grotto. Such an approach would have been impressive indeed: one would have come through the gatehouse to face the grand symmetrical façade of the castle, its twin north and east towers looming five storeys high and, between the two, the magnificent traceried windows of the great hall reaching through two floors.

One turret and two sides of the hexagon beyond the east tower survive in near-perfect condition, impressive in their height and the precision of their dressed stone (from quarries a couple of miles away, near Tisbury). The square-headed single-light windows on the ground floor are the original medieval ones, but the elegant triple-light windows with arched heads were inserted, like most of the windows in the castle, by Sir Matthew Arundell in the 1570s.

Fourteenth-century taste admired general symmetry, but was easy-going about the details, whereas the Elizabethans were in love with total symmetry. Arundell's new windows fulfilled two functions: they gave more light and were arranged as symmetrically as possible. He had no compunction about adding false windows for effect. The stack of three-light windows immediately to the left of the east tower, for instance, are all false, inserted at the back of the kitchen chimney stack.

❶ ENTRANCE ❷ PORTER'S LODGE ❸ STORE

The entrance with its rusticated columns also dates from Arundell's modernization, as do the pilastered, shell-headed alcoves in which waiting visitors could sit, his coat-of-arms over the door, and the bust of Christ in a niche above. These details, in the most up-to-date classical taste of the time, were probably designed by Robert Smythson, the mason-architect who came over from his enlargement of nearby Longleat to oversee Arundell's work. The Latin inscription below the coat-of-arms, dated 1578, recites the history of Sir Matthew and his father, and that below the bust of Christ (now hardly legible, but originally gilded) marks Sir Matthew's recovery of Wardour (see pages 30–31). Higher up are the remains of machicolations, built out over the entrance.

On both sides of the archway are the great iron pins on which the entrance doors would have hung. Originally there would have been doors and a portcullis at each end of the entrance passage. The groove from which the inner portcullis descended is still visible; the outer one was removed by Arundell when he remodelled the entrance. Beyond the broken wall of the passage are the remains of a room that was

Top: One of the classical alcove seats of the 1570s flanking the entrance
Above: *Detail of the fan vaulting. To the left can be seen the portcullis slot and one of the great iron pins on which the door would have hung*
Left: *The entrance passage and storage room alongside it; in the 14th century the passage was spanned by fan vaulting (the earliest known secular example)*

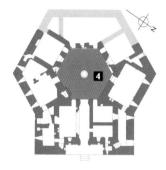

probably used for storage, as were most of the ground-floor rooms. The concrete ceiling of this room and of the entrance passage is modern, but under it at each end of the passage are the remains of the original fan vaulting of the 1390s. Such vaulting had been pioneered for some decades in English churches, but this is its first use in a secular context. It was to reach its apogee about a century later in King's College Chapel, Cambridge, and in Henry VII's chapel at Westminster Abbey.

The doorway to the right leads to what was originally the lodge where a porter would constantly have been on duty. The space at one end has a gun loop, through which he may also have questioned applicants for admittance when the doors were closed. Also in this space are the remains of his latrine. It would have had a stone shaft dropping into a horizontal drain, forming part of the elaborate system of latrines, shafts and drains which honeycombs the castle.

4 COURTYARD

The dark passage leads into the lightness of the hexagonal courtyard. Before the 1644 explosion (see page 39) brought nearly half the walls down, the courtyard would have been much darker, though impressive in height. Above the passage are the huge 14th-century inner windows of the great hall and

Above: The partly exposed fragments of a 14th-century window, in the wall opposite the entrance, blocked up during Arundell's alterations of the 1570s because it was asymmetrical
Right: *The courtyard from the east. At its centre is the 14th-century well, in which have been found various objects, dropped or discarded over centuries by the inhabitants of the castle*

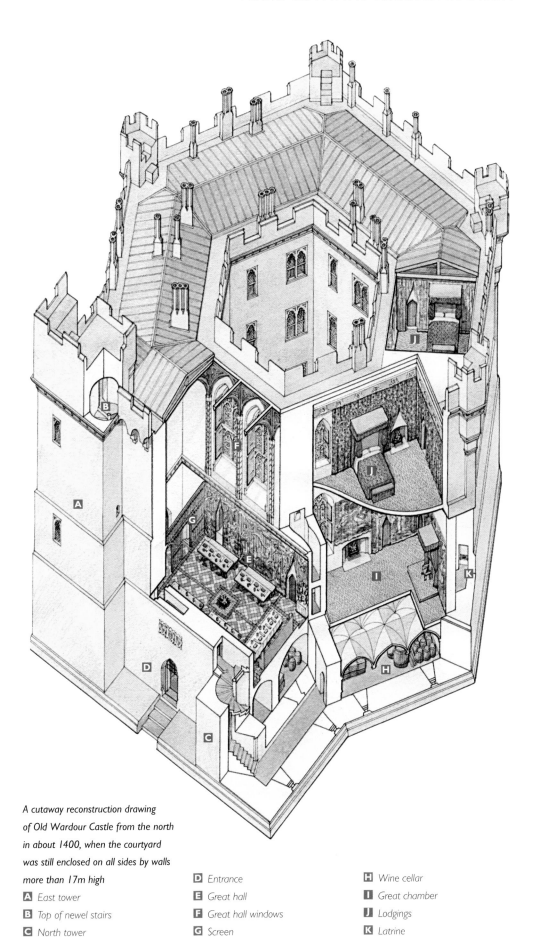

A cutaway reconstruction drawing
of Old Wardour Castle from the north
in about 1400, when the courtyard
was still enclosed on all sides by walls
more than 17m high

A East tower

B Top of newel stairs

C North tower

D Entrance

E Great hall

F Great hall windows

G Screen

H Wine cellar

I Great chamber

J Lodgings

K Latrine

Right: *The medieval door, studded with nails, that leads to the storeroom beside the entrance passage*
Below: *This woman's linen mantle, of 1600–1630, was passed down in the Arundell family and said to have been found in the well with other objects hidden there for safekeeping during the Civil War siege. It is now in the Victoria and Albert Museum, London*

to the right of these on the next side of the hexagon another pair of 14th-century windows, tall and narrow, which light the first-floor kitchen. Of the three damaged sides opposite the entrance, two have largely been demolished but the third is complete and retains its impressive stack of four sets of Arundell's three-light windows. The other two sides would have been similarly arranged to make the three sides symmetrical.

The entrance archway and the two arched openings to either side of it date from the 14th century. That on the right (facing back towards the entrance) still has its wooden medieval door. It leads into the vaulted room, probably originally a storeroom, seen from the entrance passage. At its far end a doorway gives access to the east tower newel (spiral) staircase and the rooms which it served. Immediately off the stairs to the right is a small room lit by a narrow medieval window. It was probably also used for storage.

The archway to the left of the entrance gives access to a vaulted room now used for functions and inaccessible.

5 Well

The round grille in the centre of the courtyard covers the shaft of a well. Before piped water was introduced in the 16th century this was the only source of water inside the castle enclosure. As is often the case with wells, when no longer used it became a convenient dump, and many pieces of 16th- and 17th-century pottery and the fragments of a great 16th-century alabaster chimney piece have been recovered from it.

⑥ WINE CELLAR AND ⑦ LOWER KITCHEN

Two archways – that to the right of the grand entrance that leads to the great hall, and its counterpart on the opposite side of the courtyard to the north – give access to two rooms, originally vaulted. The one to the north has no fireplace, and was almost certainly a wine cellar in Elizabethan times, and perhaps during the medieval period as well.

Wine was a luxury drink for the upper classes, and wine cellars were often elaborately treated as a result. Beer, for the main household, was probably stored in one of the other, more simply vaulted, rooms on this floor. The putative wine cellar (as well as the room to its right) is now used for functions and not normally open to the public, but through the grille can be seen the remains of its vaulting, which originally sprung from columns, two in the centre and the others round the perimeter; the effect must have been of considerable beauty.

The room opposite, on the eastern side of the courtyard, always had a chimney piece, though it has been reduced at some time from its original large size. It may have been a supplementary kitchen to the great kitchen on the floor above, perhaps used in the absence of the lord, when the full household was not in residence. Ribs from a central column, no longer existing, would have sprung to the surviving bracketed-out capitals, of unusual design, around the walls. An opening on the north side of the room, now barred, looks down into two small cellars at a lower level. These once gave access to an underground tunnel (now blocked) leading into the castle from the outside, and through which provisions could be brought into the castle and rubbish taken out, perhaps to prevent the main entrance being put to an unsuitable use.

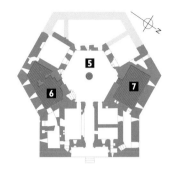

Below: Barrels of wine and beer would have stood in the ground-floor storerooms at Wardour. In this Italian manuscript of about 1470 a servant fills a jug with cider from a barrel

Bottom: The wine cellar at Wardour. Originally vaulting from columns at the centre of the room sprang to meet that fanning out from the columns around the walls

Right: The frontispiece of the Lovell Lectionary. It was completed between 1400 and 1410 by the Dominican monk and artist John Siferwas, who is here shown presenting the lectionary to Lord Lovell

Below: John, Lord Lovell and his wife, Maud, richly dressed in robes lined with ermine, portrayed in the margin of the lectionary as observers to the events depicted. The scroll held by Lord Lovell reads 'Pray for us, all saints of God'

'Pray for the soul of John, Lord Lovell, who bequeathed this book to the cathedral church of Salisbury, in special memory of him and his wife'

The Lovell Lectionary

This lectionary — a manuscript selection of passages from the Gospels — survives only in partial form, in the British Library. A Latin inscription on the frontispiece translates as 'Pray for the soul of John, Lord Lovell, who bequeathed this book to the cathedral church of Salisbury, in special memory of him and his wife'.

The lectionary is the work of the Dominican monk and artist John Siferwas, who in its frontispiece appears to depict himself presenting the lectionary to Lord Lovell. Another manuscript by him, the Sherborne Missal, similarly contains a portrait of the Abbot of Sherborne; the two are very early examples of portraiture in England. The Lovell frontispiece may have been designed in deliberate reference to the architecture of Wardour Castle:

the two traceried windows are reminiscent of its hall windows, the winding inscription of its newel stairs; and the opening at which Lord Lovell sits is so similar to Arundell's windows as to suggest that Arundell's windows were based on ones already there.

As the inscription records, the lectionary was destined for presentation to Salisbury Cathedral, where one of Richard II's inner circle, Richard Medford or Mitford, was the bishop; but it may have remained in use at Wardour until Lord Lovell's death. Its text is lavishly decorated with foliage, heraldry, animals, angels and fabulous beasts, and, as the only surviving artefact used or commissioned by Lord Lovell, can give some idea of the richness of Wardour's medieval contents.

8 LODGINGS

The three doorways on the sides of the hexagon opposite the entrance front gave access to 'lodgings': single, double or triple sets of rooms assigned to guests or members of the household according to rank. Before a corridor system was developed such lodgings usually had doors opening onto a courtyard on the ground floor (as at Wardour), or a staircase if above. The system still exists in many Oxford and Cambridge colleges.

Though the doorways remain, the rooms behind them were damaged or destroyed in the Civil War. The room to the west has all but gone, but its latrine survives in the little space once opening off it. It was clearly designed for family or guests, being on a grander scale than the latrine in the porter's lodge.

The set of lodgings on the south side of the courtyard is reached by leaving the courtyard and turning left. Here the remains give a good idea of the 'stacking' of the lodgings, and the way the newel staircase gave access to them. By 1605 the ground-floor room had become a muniment room, 'the chamber beneath the conduit where the evidence [documents] boxes stand', with a bed for the servant or clerk in charge to guard the leases and charters in the evidence boxes at night.

'The conduit' in the room above was perhaps a lead water tank, to which Arundell's two-mile-long lead piping brought water from a higher source (this was pillaged for its lead by the Parliamentarians in the Civil War, and never renewed). Pressure from the higher source forced the water along the pipe and up to the first floor, though the exact route is not known. Two prominent stone brackets at high level may have supported a beam added to bear the weight of the tank. Even higher up, in what was the uppermost chamber, are the remains of a carved chimney piece of the 1570s.

Above: This chimney piece in the south-eastern lodgings, probably one of many built for Sir Matthew Arundell in the 1570s, is the only one that survives in situ

Below: A medieval lodging, illustrated in a late 15th-century French manuscript, such as would have existed at Old Wardour

⑨ GREAT HALL

The most prominent feature in the courtyard is the great archway, framed in columns and entablature of classical Doric architecture. It was installed by Sir Matthew Arundell, to replace an earlier arch and mark the stairs leading in a graceful curve up to the great hall, and was designed and possibly carved by Robert Smythson. The lion heads on its pedestals are similar to those on the new façades at Longleat, where Smythson was doing work for Sir Thomas Thynne. Above the upper part of the staircase to the hall is perhaps the most beautiful detail at Wardour, the little 14th-century rib vault with its central boss of swirling foliage (see page 14).

The Household at Table

The hall was the grandest room at Wardour. It provided the splendid setting in which Lord Lovell, his family and guests could eat and be served with ceremony on a dais, or platform, and look down at the rows of servants and tenantry eating below them. Only its shell now survives. The four great windows, which have lost most of their tracery, are framed by slender columns that once supported the trusses of what must have been an elaborate timber roof, and beneath them runs a richly carved cornice that once divided the walls.

Above the cornice the wall may have been ornamented with painted decoration, while below it was covered with hangings; there was a similar arrangement on a grander scale at Westminster Hall in London, Richard II's masterpiece and the contemporary of the hall at Wardour. At the upper end of the hall the cornice is higher than on the other three walls to mark the raised position of the dais that would have been below it.

Hangings were replaced in the 16th century by wooden panelling. At the same time an arched wooden screen, with a gallery above it from which musicians could play, was inserted where the staircase came up; the line where the 14th-century moulding was hacked away to accommodate it can be seen. Panelling and gallery were fixed by means of wooden plugs, the square holes for which are still to be seen in the walls.

There is a variety of openings all round the hall. Two 14th-century doors at the east end lead into the service rooms

Above: Detail of the classical doorway, added by Sir Matthew Arundell in the 1570s at the entrance from the courtyard to the stairs to the great hall
Below: A typical medieval aristocratic dining scene: the guests are arranged hierarchically from the centre and waited on by menservants (from a 15th-century French manuscript)

Facing page: View of the great hall from the upper lodgings of the east tower. The huge 14th-century windows, which spanned two storeys, would have flooded the hall with light

Above right: The east end of the great hall. The square holes once held beams that supported the gallery
Above: Central boss of the rib vault above the stairs to the hall
Below: Anne Arundell (b.1615), Sir Matthew's granddaughter. As a child she would have been familiar with Wardour. She went on to found the state of Maryland in the United States with her husband, Lord Baltimore

(see page 18). Matching openings opposite each other in the sides of the hall give access to the narrow spaces into which the portcullises could be raised through slots that are still visible.

Towards the northern end of the inner wall is the chimney piece, dating in its present form from the 1570s, and in the north wall pointed Gothic archways lead to the newel staircase in the north tower (on the right), and to the great chamber and another newel staircase (on the left). These date from Lord Lovell's time, whereas the round-arched opening is an insertion of the 1570s; its position shows that by that date the dais had been removed and so suggests that Arundell seldom, if ever, ate in the hall. The sloping grooves in the walls at either end of the hall are said to have supported a temporary roof, perhaps put up when the ruinous castle was still in partial use after the Civil War, and when there was no hall floor.

⑩ GREAT CHAMBER (GREAT PARLOUR)

The archway on the left of the great hall leads past the newel staircase to a great chamber, a room which developed in importance from the 14th century onwards as the place in which the lord increasingly chose to take his meals, away from the household in the hall but still in state and ceremony. At Wardour it rose two storeys, as does the great hall. It must have been richly decorated, but little remains of it today; one wall has gone completely, and the position of the chimney piece is visible, but no more. A doorway at the end of the room leads to a latrine similar to the one on the floor below, and beyond it are the remains of a newel staircase going up.

The use and furnishing of this part of the castle in medieval times are not known, but an inventory gives a clear idea of how they were arranged in 1605. Matthew Arundell had initiated a total reordering. The medieval great chamber became the Elizabethan great parlour. Such a parlour, a type of room almost unknown in the 14th century, served as a kind of common room in which the family and their upper servants met, gossiped,

played cards or backgammon, and embroidered. Beyond the great parlour were a withdrawing parlour (more private room off the parlour) and the family's own private chambers.

Matthew Arundell moved the great chamber to a new position above the great parlour, as part of a magnificently appointed state apartment. Beyond it were the withdrawing chamber, gallery, and a series of chambers for potential important guests, from the monarch downwards. All must have had big windows and splendid views, and were filled with contents as sumptuous as any in England at the time.

Above: A 16th-century Flemish chamber. At Wardour the staterooms were similarly hung with tapestries, paintings and gilded leather
Below left: Remains of the fireplace in the great chamber
Below: A massive alabaster column of the chimney piece made for one of Matthew Arundell's vanished second-floor staterooms

Right: Lord Lovell would have taken his meals in the great chamber, when not eating with the rest of the household in the hall. In this early 16th-century Flemish manuscript illustration, a great man is waited on by his menservants at his private table before the fire
Below: Detail from a 15th-century French manuscript of a servant pouring water into a dish

The Household

The younger gentlemen servants were often related to their master and as fancifully dressed as he was

The households of great men in the 14th and 15th centuries could run to several hundred people, but, judging by the size of the hall at Wardour, Lord Lovell's is unlikely to have amounted to more than a hundred. Apart from a handful of women working for the owner's wife or children, such households were exclusively male. As with officers, non-commissioned officers and other ranks in the Army today they were divided into three groups: gentlemen, yeomen and 'others'.

The gentlemen servants were headed by the steward, who ran the whole household. He was an important and dignified figure of mature age. More decorative were the younger gentlemen servants. They were often related to their master and as fancifully dressed as he was. They waited on him at table, rode out with him when he travelled or went to war, and played backgammon with him in the evenings.

The yeomen servants included the chief cook, the usher of the hall (who kept order in the hall), the yeoman of the buttery (who looked after and served the beer), and the yeoman of the cellar (who was in charge of the wine and plate). The other ranks ranged from the waiters, who carried the food in procession to the lord's table (although the gentlemen actually served it), to the scullions, the lowest of all, filthy from smoke from the great chimney pieces and probably sleeping near the warmth of the embers on the kitchen floor.

The bigger rooms were hung with tapestry, the smaller with gilded leather. Bed curtains, chair covers and cushions were embroidered in silk and gold. There were tables inset with marble, no fewer than 166 pictures (a great rarity in an Elizabethan house), and a storeroom crammed with oriental porcelain (an even greater rarity). Hanging in the gallery was an ostrich egg. It was probably in the Elizabethan great chamber that there stood 'one extraordinary chimney piece valued at £2000' that was smashed to bits with poleaxes by Parliamentary soldiers in 1643. Many fragments of this have been recovered from the bottom of the well (see illustration page 15).

Below left: The small fireplace in the lobby, possibly Lord Lovell's private study, where he would have sat beneath the light of the window

▥ LOBBY

The little corridor beyond the upper end of the hall was in the 14th century a self-contained chamber, perhaps Lord Lovell's own study or oratory. The chimney piece in the window recess was probably inserted later, perhaps in the 15th century, but certainly before Matthew Arundell's time, for he turned the room into a corridor to provide a worthy approach to his new great chamber on the second floor. He closed off access through the rather pokey archway in the hall to the upper flights of the newel stair in the north tower and put in a new doorway where the dais had been. This opened onto what was now a wide corridor leading to the new great parlour on one side and on the other to a new flight of stairs giving a spacious link to an enlarged newel staircase up to the great chamber. The remains of the staircase are still visible, though its upper part no longer exists.

The Gallery in 1605

'In the Gallery one great looking glass on a frame, one little style [steel?] glass, one Turkey Bow with a quiver of arrows, an Indian weapon, an Indian ruff, one Coconut, a shell of the mother of pearl, 86 pictures of small and great, with the poets and pictures made in Alabaster, five maps somewhat old, one little ladder under the great glass, and an ostridge egg hanging in the middle of the Gallery.'

Above: A coconut cup made in England, 1580–1600; and below it a description in the inventory of 1605 of the gallery, which was destroyed in the Civil War

Top: The lead lion head to the right of the kitchen windows; it held in position a pipe that led from the roofs down the wall to a water tank
Above: The corner of the kitchen beside the window alcove. The archway leads via stairs to a little room that may have been the chief cook's bedchamber

🄬 BUTTERY AND 🄭 SERVERY

Two archways at the staircase end of the hall lead to what must have been the buttery, or butlery, where the yeoman of the buttery (the ancestor of the modern butler) handed out the beer brought up the newel stairs from the beer cellar; and the servery (on the right), where the waiters would collect dishes of food handed through the still-existing hatch from the kitchen. If the food was destined for the 'high table', they would organize themselves into a procession and go out through the screens into the hall (where any occupants would stand up in honour of the lord's food), and to the dais, or even further, through or up to the great chamber.

Remains of two small spaces partitioned off from the servery in the 16th century, perhaps for storage of cutlery, linen, or condiments, can be seen opposite the door.

🄮 KITCHEN AND 🄯 COOK'S CHAMBER

The door in the corner of the servery opens onto a kitchen three storeys high and lit by the two tall 14th-century windows seen from the courtyard. The walls ahead and to the left were largely or wholly filled with huge fireplaces; remains of their flues are prominent above them. When both fires were lit the room must have been appallingly hot, in spite of its height, and the scullions probably worked near-naked.

Boiling was by means of cauldrons suspended above the fires, and roasting by a spit or spits turned by the scullions. Baking was in round brick-lined ovens; the possible remains of one can be seen to the left of the main fireplace. Behind these remains runs the down shaft from the latrine on the floor above. Through an archway on the window side, narrow stairs lead up to a small room (possibly the cook's chamber), and on, by a later extension, to the gallery above the screens in the hall.

The room beyond the kitchen was originally a separate chamber. In the 16th century, when piped water was available, it was joined to the kitchen and perhaps used as a scullery, with water piped in from the conduit tank next door. A lead lion head of the 1570s can be seen from the courtyard to the right of the kitchen windows. A downpipe fixed to it probably channelled rainwater from the roofs into another tank by the kitchen door; both have long since been removed.

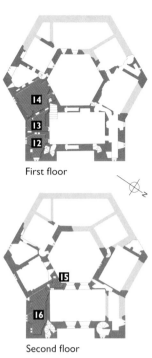

First floor

Second floor

The main fireplace in the kitchen

A *Main flue*

B *Remains of the brick-lined oven*

C *Latrine shaft*

16 EAST TOWER LODGINGS

The east tower newel stairs lead past the buttery to rooms on the second, third and fourth floors, now with concrete floors. Matthew Arundell's windows admit plenty of light today, but originally the rooms were probably plastered or limewashed and even lighter. The second-floor room has a fireplace, but no latrine, which suggests it was not a lodging. It may have been the 'wardrobe', a room used in medieval and Elizabethan times for storage and repair of fabrics such as hangings and cushions, rather than clothing. In the 16th century a doorway was inserted to give access to the gallery over the hall screens.

The third- and fourth-floor rooms, with fireplaces, latrines and inner chambers overlooking the courtyard, may have been lodgings for senior members of the household. The shaft from the third-floor latrine, between the windows, is blocked, but

Below: Scullions work in a 14th-century kitchen as they would have done at Wardour: pounding with a pestle and basting, tasting and turning chickens and ducks on a spit in the tremendous heat of the great fires

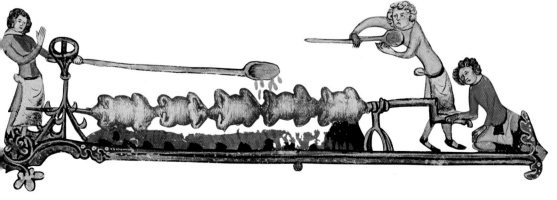

that on the fourth floor is still open. The top room is now open to the sky and its inner chamber offers the best views in the castle, down into the courtyard and kitchen, and across the lake and park to the new Wardour Castle of the 1770s. The staircase continued up to the roof and was capped by a rib vault flowering out from a central column. Even in its ruinous state this is one of the most elegant features of the castle.

⑰ NORTH TOWER STAIRCASE

At the other end of the great hall, the north tower stairs lead down to a corridor to the vaulted wine cellar. Wine would have been carried along the corridor and up the newel stairs to the high table in the hall or great chamber. In the 1570s a door to the outside in a corner of the north tower gave access to the corridor; it allowed wine and other provisions to be brought in and provided a convenient private access to the apartments as an alternative to the route through the main entrance and courtyard.

Below: The remains of the east tower newel staircase, seen from below
Bottom: *Old Wardour seen from the west, beyond the remains of the massive hexagonal outer wall. In medieval times orchards, gardens, a woodyard and stable yard would have filled the grounds around the castle*

THE GARDENS

The door in the north tower leads out onto the great lawn of the late 18th-century that slopes gently down to the outer wall. In the 14th century the slope was much steeper: the ground level on the entrance front side was much the same as today, but it dropped down to the outer wall to a level 2.5m or so below the present one, exposing much more of the wall. The levels seem to have been altered as early as the 16th century. From the wall visitors can look over to the Swan Pond, formed in the 1760s by enlarging a rectangular medieval pond. It is named from its shape, and was designed by Richard Woods, a landscape architect who worked at Wardour from 1764 to 1772.

Banqueting House

This charming little building on the outer west wall, with its gently Gothic battlements, pinnacles and double-curved ogee arches above doors and windows – features much favoured in the mid 18th century – is probably the 'banqueting room' for which payments were listed in the accounts for 1773. Its architect may have been James Paine, to whose designs the new Wardour Castle was then being built for Henry, 8th Lord Arundell. It replaced what seems to have been an earlier banqueting house of the 16th or 17th century.

The present banqueting house must originally have been intended as a place in which visitors from the new castle could take refreshments when they came to see the ruins. But the general public was probably always admitted; by the early 19th

Top: The banqueting house seen from the north. It was probably designed in the 1770s by James Paine, architect of the new Wardour Castle, which was then being built on the other side of the park

Above: The three-seater privy to the east of the banqueting house, with similar Gothic details, provided for the use of late 18th- and early 19th-century visitors

Left: Watercolour of about 1800 by Thomas Rowlandson, showing lovers admiring a picturesque scene of lake, wood and ruined castle. Taste by this time favoured the romantic and the natural over formality, and the ruins of Old Wardour below its wooded slopes were accordingly much visited

century visitors were coming in large numbers and the banqueting house was fitted up to receive them. According to a description of 1836 its main room had little tables, like a restaurant, and the small room off it was for 'any party who may wish to dine by themselves'. Refreshments were provided by an attendant who lived in its lower storey, where the public toilets now are.

The stained glass in the windows and the pretty Gothic chairs look of the same date as the banqueting house; the chimney piece is earlier and in a different style, and may have been brought in from what is now Old Wardour House (see page 41). This is the house (not open to the public) below the outer west wall, just beyond the banqueting house, in which the Arundells lived after the Civil War damage of 1644 until the building of the new castle. It was then partly demolished.

Above: A woman is brought refreshments by a manservant in the 1790s, as depicted in Thomas Rowlandson's watercolour Ladies at Tea. At Wardour refreshments were to be had in the banqueting house, where an attendant who lived in the lower storey waited on visitors
Below: The grotto, built by Josiah and Joseph Lane. According to the 19th-century garden designer JC Loudon, Josiah was paid two guineas a week, did all the work with his own hands, and was 'perfectly ignorant, but seemed to have a genius for this kind of construction'

Grotto

Further along the circuit of the outer wall is the grotto, opposite the entrance front of the castle. (The back of Old Wardour House can be seen over the wall on the way.) In front of the grotto is a terrace edged with yew trees. Terraces and clipped yews were a feature of the formal gardens laid out around the ruins in the later 17th or early 18th century, as shown in the engraving after Samuel and Nathaniel Buck (see page 40), for the occupants of the new castle. These gardens were replaced by the existing landscaping later in the 18th century.

The grotto (now partly collapsed) was built in 1792 by Josiah Lane of nearby Tisbury. Josiah and his father, Joseph, were self-taught but had a considerable reputation at the time for the construction of grottoes, which they had built at, among other places, Oatlands in Surrey, for George III's brother the Duke of York, and at Bowood (1785) and Fonthill (1794) in Wiltshire. Josiah Lane died in Tisbury Workhouse in 1835.

Standing Stones and Stone Seats

A short distance to the left of the grotto are some big standing stones, which look like more of Josiah Lane's embellishments, and beyond them two stone seats recessed in rustic stonework. This feature is probably the earlier 'grotto' (or part of it), quite different from Lane's, for which a stonemason, Haydock, was allowed to use 'old stones', presumably removed from the ruins, in about 1770. The seats are surmounted by a section of a 14th-century vault, and by what looks like the base of a 16th- or 17th-century fountain. Also lying by the seats are portions of the 14th-century columns that supported the vaults.

Stone Arch

Before leaving the castle it is worth taking the path along the outer wall behind the standing stones and the grotto. It leads to a stone arch, romantically buried in the woods. A long terrace, running over the arch, follows the contour of the hill. It was designed to give views through the trees to the ruins, as at the similar terrace above Rievaulx Abbey in Yorkshire. The terrace and arch date from the late 18th or early 19th century and are part of the 8th Lord Arundell's landscaping.

Above left: The stone arch in the woods behind the castle. The 18th-century terrace runs over the top of the arch and for a mile along the side of the hill

Top: Remains of what was probably a 16th- or 17th-century fountain base from the ruined castle, used to surmount one of the two rustic stone seats beyond the grotto

Above: One of the standing stones that may have formed part of a circle on the edge of the woods; probably another of Josiah Lane's contributions to the new romantic landscape surrounding the ruins of Wardour

History

EARLY WARDOUR

It will probably never be established whether the Wardour where King Alfred washed his hands and delivered judgement in a territorial dispute in about 900 was Wardour in Wiltshire. For practical purposes the history of Wardour begins (and that faintly enough) with the Domesday Book in 1086. In this the small manor of Wardour is recorded as being held under the king by the nuns of Wilton Abbey near Salisbury (where Wilton House now stands). For most of the 12th and 13th centuries it was tenanted or owned by the St Martin family, until sold in 1386 for £1000 by Thomas Calston, nephew and heir of Lawrence St Martin, to John, 5th Lord Lovell.

JOHN, LORD LOVELL (c.1342–1408)

Both Lord Lovell's career and the existence of Wardour Castle can largely be explained by his marriage to Maud de Holand (or Holland; c.1356–1423) in about 1372. The Lovells were a substantial baronial family, based at Minster Lovell in Oxfordshire and Tichmarsh in Northamptonshire. But they were not among the great families of England. The marriage gave them the possibility of becoming one. It was not only that Maud was an heiress. More importantly, she had good connections: her father's cousins were half-siblings to the future king.

Maud's father's uncle, Thomas de Holand, was a younger son, but he had been a successful soldier in the wars with France, and had married Joan, the daughter of Edward I's youngest son, the Earl of Kent. Thomas and Joan had two sons, Thomas and John. On de Holand's death in 1360 Joan married the Black Prince, Edward III's son and heir, and they had a son, Richard (1367–1400). Accordingly Joan's two Holand sons were the half-brothers of her son Richard, who in 1377 became Richard II and so was king when Wardour was built in the 1390s.

RISE OF THE LOVELLS

Richard succeeded his grandfather as king at the age of ten. As a boy he was overshadowed by his Plantagenet uncles and, resenting it, set out on reaching manhood to emphasize his

Facing page: Lady Lovell's cousin, John de Holand, Duke of Exeter (probably the man on the left), rides out with the Duke of Salisbury to parley on Richard II's behalf shortly before the king's fall from power in 1399, from a French manuscript of about 1401–5

Left: Detail from the Lovell Lectionary of about 1400, showing the heraldry of the Lovell and Holand families united through marriage
Below: Richard II (r.1377–99), in a detail of the Wilton Diptych, painted in the 1390s. John, Lord Lovell, who built Wardour at this time, was related to the king through marriage

divine right and to gain control of his kingdom. His Holand half-brothers supported him and profited accordingly. He rewarded them with high offices and large grants of land. He created John de Holand Earl of Huntington and Duke of Exeter, confirmed Thomas de Holand as Earl of Kent, and after Thomas's death created his son Duke of Surrey.

Richard II was to run into financial difficulties, make stupid political mistakes, fall suddenly from power in 1399, and die miserably (as Shakespeare was to depict), but for a decade he ruled as he wanted. He was not a warrior, like his father, but an aesthete, lover of luxury and patron of architecture, painting, and all the arts. It was in this decade that Wardour was built by John, Lord Lovell, the husband of his kinswoman.

As a young man Lord Lovell had been a professional soldier, and had fought across Europe and in Ireland. When Richard became king, Lovell's Holand connection took him into royal service. In 1377 he was Master of the King's Hounds; by 1378 he was a 'knight of the King's house'. By Richard's final decade he was established in the inner ring of the king's advisers and courtiers.

By appointing him governor of the royal castle in Devizes, and making him lavish grants of land in Wiltshire, the king set him up as his representative in the south-west; Lovell seems accordingly to have abandoned his Northamptonshire family castle and moved his centre of interest to Wiltshire, where, in 1393, he received from the king the 'licence to crenellate' which allowed him to build as he did at Wardour and so to establish his position as the great man in the county.

Above: Richard II (centre, holding a sceptre) shown in a late 15th-century Flemish manuscript illustration dining with two of his uncles: Thomas Woodstock, Duke of Gloucester (on the king's right) and Edmund Langley, Duke of York (on Woodstock's right). By the 1390s, when Richard was at the height of his power, Lord Lovell was part of his inner circle

With its striking hexagonal plan, traceried windows, delicately adorned vaulting and chambers with individual fireplaces and latrines, Lovell's house was the last word in grandeur, luxury and originality. Everything about it showed how close his contacts were with the court of Richard II, and how cosmopolitan and sophisticated that court was.

DESIGN OF OLD WARDOUR

The plan of Wardour shows the high-flying nature of Lovell's ambitions. It takes its place in a series of geometrically planned castles across Europe built by much greater people than he was. The sequence starts with Castel del Monte in Italy, built by the Emperor Frederick II from 1246 as an octagon with eight octagonal towers built round an octagonal court. But Wardour's prototype was the long since demolished Queenborough Castle in Kent, built by Edward III in 1361–77 as a circle within a circle within a circle, just as Wardour is a hexagon within a hexagon within a hexagon. At Wardour, however, unlike Queenborough, there was no circuit of towers, since defence was not a priority; and a plan was ingeniously worked out that combined rectangular rooms with wedge-shaped spaces at the angles, into which were fitted staircases, latrines, or small inner chambers.

To get such a plan, along with the sophisticated and elegant detail which accompanies it, Lovell must have had access to the services of one or more of the gifted master-masons who worked for the king. The two leading masons under both Edward III and Richard II were Henry Yeveley, builder and designer of Westminster Hall and much of Westminster Abbey, and William Wynford, who worked at Windsor, Winchester and Wells. The particular nature of the detail at Wardour suggests that Wynford is the most likely candidate.

It was fortunate for Lord Lovell that he was never as closely identified with Richard II as his Holand connections. When the king fell from power they fell with him, whereas John was able quietly to desert his master for the other side at the appropriate moment, and to emerge for a few years of successful if uneventful favour under Henry IV before his own death in 1408.

Above: The magnificent vaulting of the nave of Winchester Cathedral, redesigned by William Wynford in the 1390s, when he was probably also working on Old Wardour

Below: Mid 17th-century sketch by Wenceslaus Hollar of Queenborough Castle, Kent (now demolished). Built by Edward III between 1361 and 1377, it was the prototype for Wardour

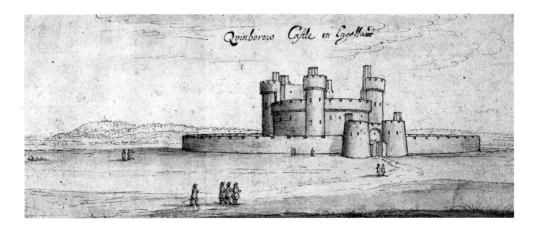

VARYING LOVELL FORTUNES

John's wife, Maud, survived him, and may have continued to live at Wardour until her death. Their eldest son, also John, died in 1414, only six years after his father, and his son, William, the 7th Lord Lovell (d.1455), inherited when still a minor. Wardour then recedes from the family picture. William's interests were concentrated on Minster Lovell, where he rebuilt the family house between about 1431 and 1442, without any of the castle imagery of Wardour. It survives today, much ruined, also in the care of English Heritage.

The family then entered on the oscillations of the Wars of the Roses, and their possessions were successively lost or recovered, as the successors of two of Edward III's younger sons, the Dukes of York and Lancaster, struggled for supremacy and the Crown. William's son John, the 8th Lord Lovell (d.1465), supported the Lancastrian Henry VI, and his estates were accordingly forfeited when Henry was deposed in 1461. He made his peace with the new king, Edward IV, and his estates were in part regranted him (although Wardour was not one of them) by the time of his death, four years later, but the family fortunes finally collapsed in the time of his son Francis.

Top: Minster Lovell, Oxfordshire, built by William, 7th Lord Lovell, between 1431 and 1442. William had shifted his interests north from Wardour, and Minster Lovell, the new family home, became the Lovells' power base from the later 15th century

Above: *Detail of the tomb of William, 7th Lord Lovell (d.1455), at St Kenelm Church, Minster Lovell*

Francis, who was born in about 1457 and so was a minor at the time of his father's death, was placed under the guardianship of Richard Neville, Earl of Warwick. The young Richard, Duke of Gloucester (1452–85), later Richard III, Edward IV's youngest brother, was also under Neville's care, possibly at the same time, at Middleham Castle. Unsurprisingly Francis became a Yorkist and supported Richard III. Francis was the Lovell of the famous doggerel naming Richard III's closest companions: 'The Cat, the Rat and Lovell our Dog, rule all

England under the Hog'. Richard made him Viscount Lovell and loaded him with grants and honours which all evaporated when Richard lost his life and his crown on Bosworth Field in 1485.

The forfeitures that followed the death of Richard III did not affect Wardour, which had remained Crown property since 1461. It went through a series of confusing changes of ownership or occupation, of no great interest as far as Wardour is concerned, for little if anything of importance happened there in those years. By 1486 the manor and castle had become the property of Thomas Butler, Earl of Ormonde, who sold it in 1499 to Robert, 1st Lord Willoughby de Broke. A series of lawsuits between Lord Willoughby's heirs were finally resolved in 1541, and in 1547 the successful heir sold the property to Sir Thomas Arundell.

THE ARUNDELLS

The Arundells were an old and well-established family of Cornish gentry, who by the 16th century had split into numerous branches, the chief of which were the Arundells of Trerice and the Arundells of Lanherne. (The fine house which John Arundell built in the 1570s at Trerice now belongs to the National Trust).

Thomas Arundell (c.1502–1552) was a younger son of Sir John Arundell of Lanherne, with his own way to make in the world. He started his career in the service of Henry VIII's chief minister, Cardinal Wolsey. He went on to become a successful government official, be appointed a Privy Councillor and acquire a knighthood and extensive property, including, in 1547, Wardour. He had married in 1530 Margaret Howard, niece of the Duke of Norfolk. Margaret's youngest sister, Catherine, became Henry VIII's fifth wife in 1541, but Thomas

Above: This silver badge of the hog, symbol of Richard III, was found on the field of Bosworth, where Francis Lovell fought alongside Richard. It would have been worn by one of Richard's knights, perhaps Lovell himself

Below: Trerice in Cornwall, the house built in the 1570s by John Arundell, head of one of the branches of the great Cornish Arundell family

Above: Elizabeth I receiving ambassadors at her court in the presence of courtiers and her ladies-in-waiting. Matthew Arundell was a courtier to Elizabeth for 26 years and married one of her ladies-in-waiting

Below: Seal on the royal grant of 1553 to Margaret Arundell, widow of the disgraced Sir Thomas, of the custody and wardship of her son Matthew and her husband's confiscated properties

was not implicated in the circumstances that led to her fall and execution in 1542. A brief connection with the Duke of Somerset, however, who ruled England as Protector during the minority of Edward VI, proved disastrous for him. Somerset was deposed by the Duke of Northumberland in 1551, and subsequently attainted of treason and executed in 1552. Sir Thomas suffered the same fate in the same year. His properties were confiscated, and although many of them were regranted to his widow, Wardour was not among them.

SIR MATTHEW ARUNDELL (1535–98)

Unlike the careers of so many of the characters who feature in Wardour's history, Matthew Arundell's was one of continuous success. He had the gift of keeping in with the people in power. He was a Catholic under Mary (r.1553–8), and a Protestant under Elizabeth (r.1558–1603), and in favour with both of them. Those of his father's forfeited properties that had been returned to his mother had been granted to her for life only, with a reversion to the Crown, but in 1554 Mary granted the reversion to him, and he inherited them when his mother died.

Matthew was in Elizabeth I's service for 26 years, and married one of her ladies-in-waiting, Margaret Willoughby. In 1597 he wrote that 'Her Majesty (I think) was scarce at any time offended with me who was as acceptable a man as any of my place or capacity'. In 1570 he bought Wardour back from the Earl of Pembroke, who then held it (and lived at Wilton, coincidentally on the site of the nunnery that had owned Wardour in the 11th and 12th centuries). He was knighted in

The Recovery of Wardour

In 1578 Matthew Arundell had an inscription carved above the entrance to Wardour Castle. It celebrated the regaining of the castle by his family after his father's downfall and loss of estates in 1552. The Latin inscription translates as follows: 'Thomas, a younger son of the Arundells of Lanherne, first

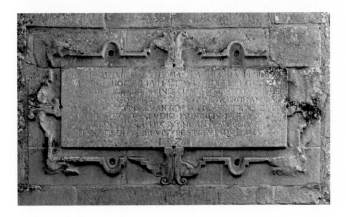

gained the right to settle in this place. As soon as he had settled he fell. He was punished although innocent and above reproach. His innocence was attested by subsequent events. For his son Matthew bought back what had been his father's, and having bought it, increased it. By the favour of the Prince it has stayed increased. I pray that it may long so remain and go on being increased for ever. What God gave and took away, he has restored. 1578'

1574, held the profitable post of Collector of Customs at Poole, and was Sheriff and Deputy Lieutenant of Dorset. Wardour was only the first of his purchases in Wiltshire, Dorset, Somerset and Devon, which led to his being listed in 1588 as one of the 12 knights 'of great possessions' worthy of being given a peerage.

Until he bought Wardour, Matthew had been living in a sizeable house at Shaftesbury built by his father (of which nothing remains). But he had no hesitation in moving from it to make Wardour his principal home. Buying it was an act of filial piety and of restitution of his father's honour, who, as his inscription at Wardour records, had been unjustly accused.

In addition Matthew knew that in buying Wardour he was buying a plum – 'the wonder of the West', as Sir John Harington, godson of Elizabeth I, was later to call it. Great medieval castles were admired by the Elizabethans, and those who lived in them were proud of them. Perhaps the most famous house (excluding royal palaces) in Elizabeth's reign was Kenilworth Castle, the medieval pile of her favourite, the great Earl of Leicester, who welcomed his queen there in 1575 with splendour at a famous entertainment that lasted 19 days (Arundell was one of those present). Leicester embellished Kenilworth with as much care for its medieval character as Arundell was to show in his work on Wardour. In addition, Wardour's hexagonal plan was just the kind of unusual and original 'device' that delighted the Elizabethans; Arundell's neighbour Sir Thomas Gorges, for instance, built his triangular

Above left: Matthew Arundell's Latin inscription of 1578 over the entrance of Wardour Castle, which celebrates the regaining of his father's castle
Above: Sir John Harington, godson to Elizabeth I and visitor of Old Wardour, which he described as 'the wonder of the West'. This portrait of about 1590 is attributed to Hieronimo Custodis

Right: The first known depiction of
Old Wardour Castle, on a survey
made for the Earl of Pembroke in
1566, four years before Matthew
Arundell bought it from him. This
fascinating but puzzling drawing
appears to show much narrower
entrance towers than are here today.
If accurate, it would mean that the
14th-century towers contained only
newel staircases, and were enlarged
by Matthew Arundell
Below: Design for a two-storey,
pilastered bay window for Longleat,
by Robert Smythson, 1570s. In the
end Longleat was built three, not two,
storeys high. It is likely that Smythson
also worked at Wardour

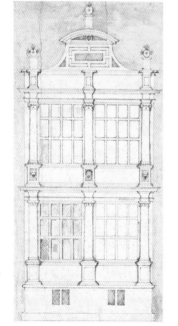

Longford Castle just a few years after Arundell's work at
Wardour. Even so, Wardour needed to be brought up to date,
and Arundell set out to modernize it, with the results already
described (see pages 14–17).

In the 1570s Sir John Thynne, another of Arundell's
Wiltshire neighbours, was busy enlarging and re-modelling his
house at Longleat to make it the most advanced and splendid
classical house in England. The work was designed and
part-executed by two masons, the Englishman Robert
Smythson and the Frenchman Alan Maynard.

In June 1576 Arundell had some beds to sell and Thynne
was interested in buying them, but was outbid by Sir William
Courtenay of Powderham Castle in Devon. In June Arundell
wrote to Thynne: 'I herd again by Smythson you would
willingly have them.' He added that he would try to persuade
Courtenay to give them up, although, he wrote, 'he [Courtenay]
said before Smythson he would not forgo them'. There is little
doubt that 'Smythson' was Robert Smythson, and that he was
at Wardour as a mason, and not just to bargain over beds.
The classical work at Wardour, especially the magnificent
portal in the courtyard, relates closely to his work at Longleat.

THE EARLY 17TH CENTURY

Matthew Arundell's contemporaries suspected him, with some
justice, of being a Catholic at heart, but one who kept in favour
with the queen and the government by outwardly conforming
to the Church of England. It was a great embarrassment to
this careful man that his brother, Charles, and his own son and
heir Thomas (*c.*1560–1639) were openly Catholic, and often
in trouble as a result.

Robert Smythson

The mason-architect Robert Smythson (1535/6–1614) was one of the creators of the Elizabethan style. Unique to England, this style was a worthy accompaniment to the literature of the age of Shakespeare, with its classical detail, huge windows of many lights, ingenious symmetrical plans and dramatic groupings of towers and gables. A large collection of drawings, some of great beauty, made by him and his son John are at the Victoria and Albert Museum, London.

Smythson was trained and probably born in London, and moved to Wiltshire in 1568. His three best-known houses were Longleat in Wiltshire (externally remodelled by him, 1572–80) for Sir John Thynne; Wollaton Hall, Nottingham

(newly built, 1580–88) for Sir Francis Willoughby; and Hardwick Hall, Derbyshire (newly built, 1590–97) for the Countess of Shrewsbury, better known as Bess of Hardwick. Sir Francis Willoughby was the brother of Matthew Arundell's wife, Margaret, and it was probably this connection which had Smythson move up to Wollaton, where he remained until his death.

It was to the credit of Smythson and Arundell that they realized that the great many-light windows of Longleat would have been out of keeping with the character of Wardour: instead they successfully modernized the castle without destroying its baronial character.

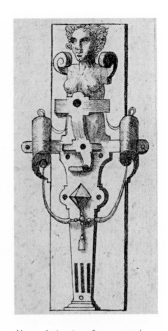

Above: *A drawing of ornamental strapwork by Smythson, one of his preparatory designs for Wollaton Hall, home of Matthew Arundell's brother-in-law, Sir Francis Willoughby* **Below:** *Longleat, by Jan Siberechts, about 1675. Robert Smythson was at work at Longleat in the 1570s, at the same time as he was employed six miles away at Wardour*

In 1595, three years before his father's death, Thomas went to fight in Hungary against the Turks. He had the queen's encouragement, for the aggressive and expanding Turkish empire was seen as the great threat to Christian Europe, and Christians of all denominations joined to fight against it.

Thomas fought with such outstanding bravery that in reward he was created a Count of the Holy Roman Empire by the Emperor Rudolf II of Austria. He accepted the honour without consulting his own queen. Elizabeth was furious, not so much because it was a Catholic honour given by a Catholic monarch but because it impugned her own authority. As she put it (according to the historian William Camden), 'I would not have my sheep branded with another man's mark.' Thomas was in trouble, and out of favour for the rest of her reign. He got on better under James I (r.1603–25), and in 1605 finally achieved an English peerage for his family, being created Baron Arundell of Wardour.

Above: Helmet, now hanging in Tisbury church, said to have been worn by Thomas Arundell when he fought, with great bravery, in Hungary

Plumbing at Wardour

Wardour, like other great 14th-century houses and castles, had an elaborate sanitary system. The more important chambers had their own latrines letting onto vertical down shafts throughout the castle. These connected with two vaulted main drains running out of the castle and down the hill. Many of the down shafts remain unidentified, however, and we do not know the position and outlets of the main drains, nor how they connected with the drains inside the castle.

Although the system must have seemed the height of luxury in the late 14th century, it had its disadvantages: the shafts honeycombing the walls reduced their strength and contributed to their collapse in the great explosion of 1644, and both down shafts and drains were likely to foul up

and smell. At some houses, in the 14th century and later, rainwater was fed off the roof into the shafts in an attempt to wash them out. There may have been some such device at Wardour, but it has not been traced.

Perhaps it was the malodorous failure of the system that led to a discussion at Wardour in or about 1592. Sir John Harington, who invented the water closet, and described and illustrated it in his *Metamorphosis of Ajax*

Above: Latrine off the medieval great chamber on the first floor at Wardour
Above right: Henry Wriothesley, later 3rd Earl of Southampton, in about 1592, about the time he attended a dinner at Old Wardour with his sister, at which the novel concept of a water closet was discussed

Thomas went on to disobey royal orders as a newly appointed colonel in the army, was suspected of involvement in the Gunpowder Plot of Guy Fawkes, married for the second time at the age of 40, was caught up in religious argument with the Bishop of Durham and finally attempted to sell Wardour back to the king in 1637. He died in 1639, leaving his son Thomas to live on uneventfully at Wardour until the outbreak of the Civil War in 1642 introduced the most violent two years in the castle's history.

CIVIL WAR: THE TWO SIEGES OF WARDOUR
The Arundells lose Wardour: 1643

The Civil War was the culmination of a long struggle between James I's successor, Charles I (r.1625–49), and Parliament (especially the House of Commons), as Parliament tried to increase its powers at the expense of the king's, and the king resisted. War finally broke out in August 1642. It was to evoke

Above: Thomas, 1st Baron Arundell of Wardour, painted by Anthony van Dyck in the early 1630s

(1596), relates how the device was 'first thought of and discoursed of' by six people, in 'a castle that I call the wonder of the West'. A copy annotated by him (now in the Folger Library, Washington), reveals that the castle was Wardour, and that the six people were Harington himself, Sir Henry Danvers, Sir Matthew Arundell, his son Thomas, his son's wife, Mary, and her brother the Earl of Southampton (in all probability the young man to whom Shakespeare addressed many of his sonnets).

In fact Harington's water closets did not work very well. One was installed in a royal palace (Harington was Elizabeth I's godson), one in the Earl of Salisbury's house in London, and presumably one in Harington's own house, near Bath, but the invention failed to catch on, until improved in the late 17th century. If one was installed at Wardour, there is no trace of it there today.

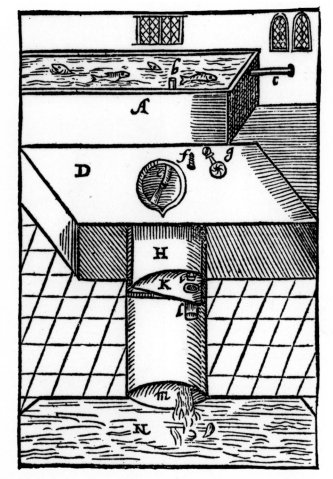

Above: Harington's 1596 design for a water closet includes the cistern (A), waste pipe (C), seat (D), cistern pipe (E), 'screw' (F), 'scallop shell to cover it [the screw]' (G), 'stool pot' (H), sluice (L), and 'vault into which it falls' (N)

violent partisanship, and to divide neighbour from neighbour and, on occasion, father from son and brother from brother. But the Catholics, always favoured by Charles and distrusted by Parliament, were solidly behind the king.

In the spring of 1643 Thomas, 2nd Lord Arundell (c.1586–1643), went to Oxford to join the king, who had his headquarters there, leaving his 60-year-old wife, Blanche, at Wardour, with little but the male members of the household to protect her. The Parliamentarians may have seen the castle as a potential threat if properly garrisoned, and certainly believed that it contained great wealth in plate and money, which they could commandeer for their cause. On 2 May 1643, Sir Edward Hungerford, the local Parliamentary commander, came to occupy it. He may have expected little resistance, but in fact Blanche refused him entry, saying that 'She had a command from her Lord to keep it', and the first siege of Wardour began.

There are two accounts of this siege, one by the Royalist clergyman Bruno Ryves, the other in the memoirs of Edmund Ludlow, who arrived at Wardour with a supporting troop of Parliamentary cavalry in the last days of the siege, and stayed to garrison it. Not surprisingly, the Royalist account stresses the heroism of the tiny garrison, blazing away at the enemy while the maidservants, 'valiant beyond their sex', helped them load and reload their muskets. Ludlow's account is more restrained.

Above: *Thomas, 2nd Lord Arundell, a 19th-century engraving based on an earlier miniature. Thomas was fatally wounded at the Battle of Stratton, near Oxford, in 1643*

Right: *Frontispiece of the Royalist Bruno Ryves's news booklet,* Mercurius Rusticus, *in which he describes the valiant defence of Wardour by Lady Blanche and her small garrison, despite their being 'distracted' with hunger and lack of sleep*

Lady Blanche: the Defence of Wardour

Lady Blanche Arundell (1583/4–1649) was the daughter of Edward Somerset, 4th Earl of Worcester. The Somersets lived at Raglan Castle in Monmouthshire, even more magnificent than Wardour, and like it besieged in the Civil War. Blanche was one of several wives who were left at home when their husbands went off to fight, and bravely defended their castles or fortifiable houses.

Mary, Lady Bankes, together with a string of daughters and a garrison of 80, resisted the Parliamentary besiegers of Corfe Castle, Dorset, for six weeks in the summer of 1643, though she was forced to surrender on a second siege in 1646. A garrison of 300, commanded by the formidable French-born Countess of Derby (in male military gear, according to – possibly malicious – Parliamentary accounts), defended Lathom House in Lancashire for three months in 1644.

The Parliamentary counterpart to these gallant Royalist women was Brilliana, Lady Harley, who with equal success defended Brampton Bryan Castle in Herefordshire for six weeks in 1643. In this company Blanche Arundell's six days' resistance might seem unimpressive; but her age, tiny garrison, and the sympathetic account of Bruno Ryves caught the imagination of romantically inclined writers in the 19th century, and she became the best-known member of the Arundell family.

Above: An engraving of 1841 showing Lady Blanche directing the defence of Wardour while Sir Thomas Arundell is away fighting for the king

Below: A 17th-century portrait of Charlotte de la Tremouille, Countess of Derby, tearing up the summons to surrender Lathom House in defiance. Charlotte defended Lathom from the Parliamentarians for three months

Twenty-five men in the castle, armed with muskets, were faced by a force (according to the Royalist account) of 1,300. But the besiegers only had two small cannon. These had little effect on the castle walls, apart from one ball bursting through a window and damaging a chimney piece. Having got nowhere with their cannon the besiegers tried letting off barrels of gunpowder, first in a tunnel leading to the castle, and then in one of the two main drains. The first explosion had no effect, and the second shook the castle but did little damage; it worked its way, however, through the interconnecting shafts of the sewage system, and the blasts of hot air from the latrines greatly alarmed the defenders.

The Parliamentarians then inserted further barrels of gunpowder, set an hour-glass in motion, and threatened another, and probably bigger, explosion if the castle were not surrendered before the hour-glass ran out. According to Ludlow, the threat 'so terrified the ladies therein, whereof there was a great number, that they agreed to surrender it' on 8 May 1643. The castle was pillaged, much damage done in the park and wood, and the great chimney piece smashed, together with numerous 'rare pictures … a loss that neither cost nor art can repair'. After being taken as prisoner to Shaftesbury Blanche was allowed to take refuge in Salisbury, where she was soon to learn that her husband had died on 19 May of wounds received three days earlier at the Battle of Stratton near Oxford.

Above: Effigy of Sir Edward Hungerford on his tomb at the family home, Farleigh Hungerford Castle. Sir Edward is shown in full armour, holding the commander's baton. While he led the Parliamentarian forces against Wardour, his half-brother John held Farleigh Hungerford Castle for the Royalists

Right: Henry, 3rd Lord Arundell of Wardour. Henry is shown wearing a breastplate and holding his baton as Master of the Horse to Henrietta Maria, the Queen Mother, to which position he was appointed in 1663

Facing page, top: Wardour from the south-west, showing the damage caused by the accidental explosion of barrels of gunpowder beneath the castle walls

The Arundells regain Wardour: 1643–4

The castle now in the possession of the Parliamentarians, Edmund Ludlow moved in with his troop of cavalry and a company of infantry as a garrison. He remained there until the end of the year, when Blanche Arundell's son, Henry (1607/8–1694), now the 3rd Lord Arundell, came with a large force to retake it.

The second siege lasted from December 1643 until March 1644 and, with a sizeable garrison opposed to besiegers with bigger cannon, was a much more formidable affair. Even so, the castle, although much battered, was only taken when an engineer was brought in, supported by miners from the Mendips lead mines.

A shaft was dug under the castle walls, and a gunpowder mine laid ready for firing. It is likely that Henry Arundell was none too willing to destroy his own castle, and may have hoped that Ludlow would surrender before this proved necessary. In fact the mine seems to have been set off by mistake, by a shot from the defenders. Ludlow was in bed, and woken up by the explosion to find, as in an earthquake, that a large chunk of his bedroom wall had disappeared. After a three-day attempt to storm access through the gap the besiegers dug a second mine, at the threat of which Ludlow finally surrendered, on 18 March 1644.

Below: The conditions of surrender of Wardour Castle by Lady Blanche, signed and sealed by Sir Edward Hungerford and his deputy, William Strode. It states that the women and their servants shall 'have their lives and all fitting respect due to persons of their sex and quality'

Above: An unexecuted design of the 1760s by Richard Woods for the rebuilding and restoration of Old Wardour for the 8th Lord Arundell

Below: Engraving of Old Wardour from the south-east, by Samuel and Nathaniel Buck, 1732. The formal gardens of clipped hedges and topiary were probably done away with by Richard Woods in the 1760s, when he did extensive work on the gardens

ABANDONMENT AND RETURN

Having blown up his castle in order to recover it, Henry Arundell was not allowed to keep it for very long. As a result of the final victory of Parliament in 1648, followed by the execution of Charles I in 1649, Wardour Castle was surrendered and the estates of the Arundell family were confiscated. Henry recovered the bulk of his estates when the monarchy was restored and Charles II became king in 1660, but he made no attempt to restore the shattered castle. Under James II, at the age of about 80, he rose to the position of Lord Privy Seal. He had removed to Hampshire, where he rented an Elizabethan mansion, Breamore House (now open to the public), kept a famous pack of hounds and died in 1694.

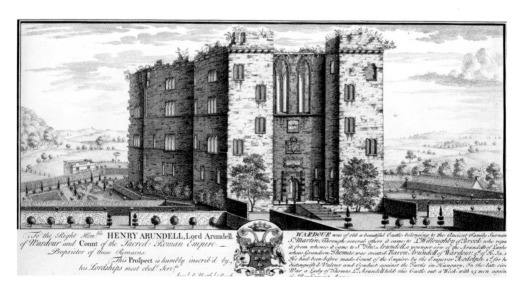

Existing buildings south of the outer castle wall were fitted up for Henry's occasional visits. These were enlarged and improved by succeeding generations to become what is now Old Wardour House. Although the castle was left a ruin, elaborate gardens in the formal taste of the time were laid out round it, perhaps based on what had been there before the Civil War. The engraving of the castle made by Samuel and Nathaniel Buck in 1732 shows the clipped topiary yew trees which were their most prominent feature.

Meanwhile, for three generations discussions went on over what to do about a new house. The house by the castle was a makeshift; a new and grander house was needed for a family of the wealth and status of the Arundells. But should it be built on the site of the old castle, and the ruins destroyed, or on a new site altogether?

NEW WARDOUR CASTLE

The young Henry, 8th Lord Arundell (1740–1808), whose portrait of about 1765 by Reynolds so splendidly combines opulence and informality, was to inaugurate a new era at Wardour, as important as those of Lord Lovell and Sir Matthew Arundell. He had inherited at the age of 16 from his father, the 7th Lord Arundell (1717–56), the considerable Arundell estates. The seventh lord had increased his estates through marriage and inheritance: in 1739 he had married his kinswoman, Mary Arundell of Lanherne, heiress to the ancestral Arundell estates in Cornwall and elsewhere, and in 1753 he inherited valuable properties at the eastern end of Piccadilly in London from his childless Panton uncle, whose sister had

Above: Portrait of Henry, 5th Lord Arundell, his wife, Elizabeth Panton, and their children Henry, Thomas and Elizabeth. Elizabeth Panton brought considerable estates to the Arundell family, notably the area around Panton Street in London
Below: Mary Arundell of Lanherne, heiress to the Cornish Arundell estates, who married her cousin the 7th Lord Arundell in 1739

Right: Henry, 8th Lord Arundell of
Wardour (1740–1808), in about
1765, by Sir Joshua Reynolds. Henry
is shown dressed in his ceremonial
robes of state

Below: The south front of the new
Wardour Castle seen from across one
of the ponds in the park; engraved by
Letitia Byrne from a study by John
Preston Neale, and published in 1830

married his grandfather, the fifth lord (hence Panton Street in
Soho, London, but not Arundel or Wardour Streets, named
after the earls of Arundel and an Edward Wardour).

In general the Catholics were now becoming an accepted
rather than a persecuted minority, and the richer Catholic
families, who had kept a low profile in previous generations,

Above: A drawing for the new castle by James Paine, of about 1768. It is done in section through the centre of the house to show Lord Arundell the proposed design of the entrance hall, with its circular staircase, upper landing and coffered dome supported on Corinthian columns
Left: The entrance hall of the new Wardour Castle, built between 1770 and 1776, as it appears today
Below: One of the rustic alcove seats built in the 1770s as part of the romanticization of the gardens around the ruins of the old castle

had the confidence to build and plant on the grand scale. Soon after his marriage to the heiress Mary Conquest in 1763 the eighth lord took a momentous decision. He finally rejected the idea of restoring or rebuilding the old castle. Instead, he determined to build a magnificent new Wardour on a higher site a mile away. The old castle would not be demolished, but preserved as an evocative ruin, a monument to the family history, and a major feature in the park, lakes and woodland that would surround the new building (see pages 44–5).

It was 1770, however, before work on the new Wardour Castle began, though the site had probably been decided on in 1764. The architect was James Paine, chosen, in all likelihood, because he had already designed two splendid houses for Catholic clients: Worksop in Nottinghamshire for the Duke of Norfolk and Thorndon in Essex for Lord Petre.

The house which he designed for Lord Arundell, and into which Henry moved in 1776, was a splendid classical building with nothing of a 'castle' about it, except its name. It was planned round a circular domed staircase, as grand as any in England. In one of the wings was an equally magnificent private chapel, designed by Paine but enlarged to the designs of the leading architect Sir John Soane in 1788–90.

Above: Old Wardour from the west, seen from across the Swan Pond
Below: A watercolour of 1791 showing women stitching and reading on a bench in a garden. By this date the gardens at Wardour had been replanted in the naturalistic fashion, and were no doubt similarly enjoyed by their many visitors

THE PLEASURE GARDENS

By the mid 18th century the gardens of Old Wardour must have seemed painfully out of date. There had been a reaction against topiary, trimmed hedges, straight lines and geometrically arranged flower beds. A new appreciation had developed for natural beauties, for rivers, hills, mountains, lakes and woodland. Artists travelled to the Lake District and the wilder parts of Wales, and with the new taste in mind picked out the features that would make a good picture. Such landscapes were accordingly described as 'picturesque'. Ruins were considered 'picturesque' too, because of their historical associations and their irregularly broken outlines, shaggy with ivy.

Appreciation of such landscapes led to the realization that gardens and parks could be made picturesque too. A new group of designers appeared, ready to replace straight avenues with scattered clumps of trees, straight canals or rectangular ponds with winding lakes, straight paths and roads with curving ones. A genuine ruin was eagerly prized: in Yorkshire the ruins of Fountains Abbey were made the culminating feature of the pleasure grounds of Studley Royal, and the park at Duncombe

Park was extended with a long winding terrace from which to obtain views cut down through the woods to the ruins of Rievaulx Abbey. Two landscape gardeners are especially associated with Wardour, Richard Woods and Lancelot 'Capability' Brown (so nicknamed because of the ingratiating way he told prospective clients that he saw great 'capabilities' in the settings of their houses). Brown is far better known than Woods, but Woods was more important at Wardour.

The 7th Lord Arundell had commissioned a plan from Brown in 1754, but he died not long after; Brown had some difficulty in getting paid. Brown's plan has disappeared, and it is unlikely that any part of it was carried out. Instead, in 1764, the eighth lord went to Richard Woods for 'A Design for the Improvement of Wardour', which still survives.

Woods designed parks and gardens, and often buildings to go with them, for a mainly Catholic clientele. Much of his plan for Wardour was never carried out, and much has been destroyed, but his mark is still on the landscape. His most obvious contribution is the Swan Pond, which he created from the previous rectangular pond and planted round with trees. Other embellishments included a Gothic temple and an ice-house, which have disappeared, and a cold bath-house, the rusticated portico of which survives attached to part of Ark Farm nearby (not open to the public). It was probably Woods, too, who got rid of the old formal gardens round the ruins, laid down the great lawns, and planted the cedars which, to judge from their appearance in illustrations of the 1820s, are unlikely to have been planted later than his time. It is not known who was responsible for the woodland terrace and archway.

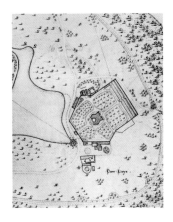

Above: Detail of a survey done for Henry, 8th Lord Arundell, in 1773, the year after Richard Woods's works were completed; it shows Woods's proposals (seen below) largely carried out

Below: Part of 'A Design for the Improvement of Wardour' by Richard Woods, 1764. It shows the rectangular pond remodelled as the Swan Pond, with an improbable sailing boat on the water

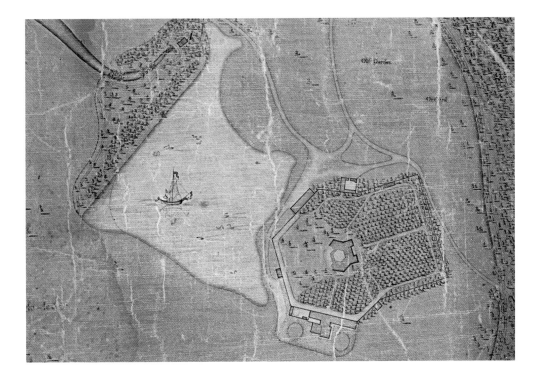

Above: James Canter's view of Old Wardour, from the 1760s or 1770s. The figures in the foreground wander among the roses and hollyhocks, and a gardener is at work to the left
Below: Mary Arundell (1757–1832), sister of James, 9th Lord Arundell, as a young woman, by Thomas Stewart. Mary would have been a visitor at Wardour, the home of her cousin the eighth lord and later of her brother

But Woods's main contribution to Old Wardour Castle is its actual existence. The seventh lord had been set to demolish it and rebuild on the same site. Woods, in a cogently argued report, made the case for building on a different site, in fact the site that was finally chosen. A new house features in outline on his plan, and he sent in at least two designs for it, both rejected by the 8th Lord Arundell. They fell out, and he dismissed himself, or was sacked, in 1772. Lord Arundell then wrote to Brown, inviting him to Wardour. Brown produced another plan for the landscape, dated 1773. Little of it seems to have been carried out, except in the immediate environs of the new house.

WARDOUR IN THE 19TH CENTURY

The eighth lord's landscaping and building were combined with lavish collecting of contents for the new house, the splendid fitting up of the new chapel, and an abundantly generous lifestyle. He had no sons, but two daughters, the elder of whom, Mary, married his cousin James. Mary died in 1805, leaving six children. When her father died three years later his estates passed to James, who became the 9th Lord Arundell.

In his will the eighth lord ruefully remarked that he was not sure that there would be money to pay his numerous legacies. In 1811 William Bankes from Kingston Lacy visited Wardour and reported that the ninth lord 'is still greatly straitened by the enormous debts contracted by his predecessor, principally in building a house quite disproportionate to his fortune'. To pay off his debts James was forced to sell land in Wiltshire, together with the greater part of the London property.

The old castle remained throughout the 19th century and beyond as the eighth lord had enhanced and embellished it, its romantic creeper-clad ruins in their verdant setting open to the public and a popular attraction for tourists.

Games Amongst the Ruins

'We used to disguise ourselves to take people in. John started it by dressing in old ragged clothes, and opening the gate for people passing through to visit the Old Castle ruins. He bowed and Blanche and I curtsied and held out our hands for pennies. They used to dirty my face and pinch me to make me look deprived. John made quite a lot of money, Blanche got half, and I was left with bruises.'

From the unpublished memoirs of Isabel, sister of John, 16th Lord Arundell

Left: Gerald, 15th Lord Arundell, his daughter Isabel, son, John, and wife, Ivy; Wardour Castle, January 1929

THE LAST LORD ARUNDELL OF WARDOUR

John (1907–44), the 16th and last Lord Arundell, grew up with his two sisters at Wardour Castle. He was a captain in the Army during the Second World War, and after arriving in France in September 1939 he was captured by the Germans while retreating with his company in May 1940. He escaped from Eichstatt prison in 1943, but was recaptured and taken to Colditz. A fellow prisoner recalled: 'I think of him being up early in the morning, taking a cold shower and jogging around

Below: A photograph taken between 1855 and 1920 of Old Wardour from the south-west. The trees planted in the late 18th century stretch nearly to the walls of the ruin, which is overgrown with ivy

the courtyard before there were many other people there. He was a gallant and much loved man.'

John was sent back to Britain in 1944, with tuberculosis. He died days after reaching British soil, in September 1944. He was 37 and unmarried, and with his death the Barony of Arundell of Wardour became extinct. In 1936 his father had handed over the old castle to the guardianship of the State, although retaining ownership. Decades of restoration and research followed: the ivy was removed from the ruins, excavations were carried out and concrete floors were installed to improve access. Today the ruins are maintained on behalf of the State by English Heritage, but are still the property of Lord Arundell's successor, Lord Talbot of Malahide, who owns most of the surrounding land.

Above: View from the east lodgings of Old Wardour, through one of Sir Matthew Arundell's three-light windows of the 1570s